G😺😺d Habits
for God's Kids
My Clean Room

written by JEAN FISCHER
illustrated by ANGELA KAMSTRA

Scripture taken from the HOLY BIBLE, NEW INTERNATIONAL VERSION®. NIV®. Copyright ™ 1973, 1978, 1984 by International Bible Society. Used by permission of Zondervan Publishing House. All rights reserved.

08 07 06 05 04 03 02 01   9 8 7 6 5 4 3 2 1

ISBN 0-7847-1223-9

Standard
Publishing
Cincinnati, Ohio

"Sara Beth, your room's a mess!" Mom said when she tucked Sara Beth into bed. "Please have it cleaned up by tomorrow afternoon."

Sara Beth looked around her room at all her favorite things: her stuffed animals, her dolls, her books, her toys. She didn't think her room was messy.

The next morning, Howard came over to play.
"Hey, Sara Beth," Howard said, "Let's ride our
bikes to the park."

But Sara Beth couldn't find her bike helmet. She
looked under her bed and inside her closet. She looked
in her toy chest and under a pile of clothes. She looked
on the bookcase and behind the door.

Sara Beth couldn't find her bike helmet, so she
didn't go to the park.

Later that morning, Oscar asked to borrow Sara Beth's goggles for his swimming lesson. But Sara Beth couldn't find her goggles. She looked under her bed and inside her closet. She looked in her toy chest and under a pile of clothes. She looked on the bookcase and behind the door.

Sara Beth couldn't find her goggles, so she couldn't share with Oscar. She felt sorry about that.

Later that day, Sara Beth heard the ice cream truck coming down the street!

"Mom!" Sara Beth cried. "Can I have money for ice cream?"

"Look in your piggy bank," Mom answered.

But Sara Beth couldn't find her piggy bank. She looked under her bed and inside her closet. She looked in her toy chest and under a pile of clothes. She looked on the bookcase and behind the door. She even looked inside an empty box of crackers.

All of Sara Beth's friends got ice cream. But Sara Beth couldn't find her piggy bank, so Sara Beth didn't get any at all.

Sara Beth flopped down on her bed. She looked around her room and cried, "My room is a terrible mess, and so am I!"

Mom came in and sat down on the bed. "You're
not a mess, sweetheart, but you are unhappy. God
has given you so many good gifts—toys, games,
books—but if you can't find them, you can't enjoy them
or share them. When you take good care of your things,
you please God, and you will be happier too."

Sara Beth stood up. She knew just what to do to please God and make herself happy.

First she cleaned under her bed. That's where she found her bike helmet.

Then Sara Beth hung up all her clothes. That's when she found her swimming goggles.

After that Sara Beth
picked up all of her books
and all of her toys.
   And that's when she
found her piggybank!

"Mom!" Sara Beth called, "Come look at my clean room!"

"Your room looks so much better, and so do you. Thank you for taking care of your things and for obeying me today by cleaning up."

Then Sara Beth and her mom went together to find the ice cream truck.

Note to Parents

Ephesians 5:15 says, "Be very careful, then, how you live—not as unwise but as wise, making the most of every opportunity." This storybook is part of a Happy Day® series designed to help children learn about the good habits of wise living. Use the following suggestions to help your children be responsible to take care of the things God has given them.

Try these tips for making clean-up a snap.

- Make clean-up time fun. Have a contest to see who can clean up the most in 15 minutes.

- Set aside a special "clean time" every day. It's easier to do a little bit of work each day instead of making it a huge job to do later.

- Get organized to make it easier to keep up with belongings and make clean-up a cinch.